I0817402

Giving An Oral Presentation

by Jeff McHugh

Go to
www.openlightbox.com
and enter this book's
unique code.

ACCESS CODE

LBXR3547

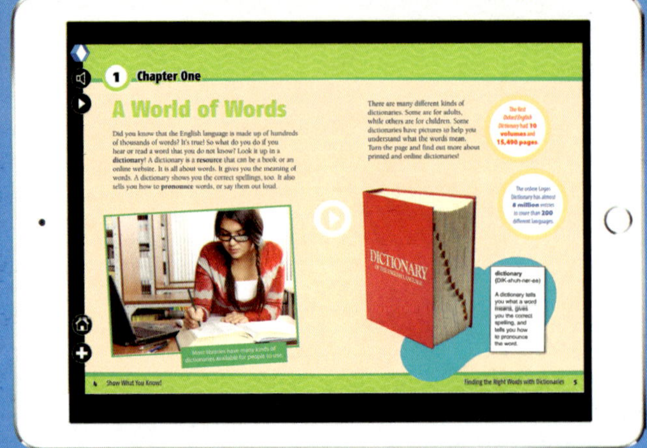

Lightbox is an all-inclusive digital solution for the teaching and learning of curriculum topics in an original, groundbreaking way. Lightbox is based on National Curriculum Standards.

STANDARD FEATURES OF LIGHTBOX

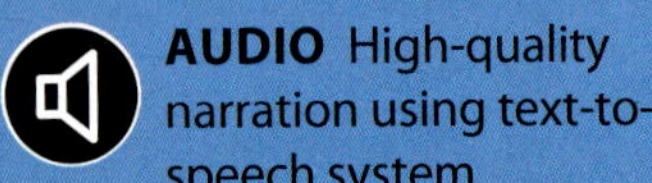

AUDIO High-quality narration using text-to-speech system

ACTIVITIES Printable PDFs that can be emailed and graded

SLIDESHOWS Pictorial overviews of key concepts

VIDEOS Embedded high-definition video clips

WEBLINKS Curated links to external, child-safe resources

TRANSPARENCIES Step-by-step layering of maps, diagrams, charts, and timelines

INTERACTIVE MAPS Interactive maps and aerial satellite imagery

QUIZZES Ten multiple choice questions that are automatically graded and emailed for teacher assessment

KEY WORDS Matching key concepts to their definitions

Giving An Oral Presentation

2 Lightbox Book Code

4 CHAPTER ONE
Getting Started

10 CHAPTER TWO
Planning Your Presentation

13 CHAPTER THREE
Research and Write

16 CHAPTER FOUR
Practice Makes Perfect

18 CHAPTER FIVE
Presentation Time!

21 Quiz

22 Key Words

23 Index

24 Log on to www.openlightbox.com

Getting Started

"Boys and girls, everyone has to give an **oral presentation**," Anita's teacher says.

Some people have no problem speaking in front of people. Others suffer stage fright!

How would you feel about speaking in front of the whole class? Some people love being in front of an audience. If you are one of these people, this book will help you improve your presentation skills. However, many people get nervous about giving oral presentations. If this sounds like you, don't worry! Use the tips in this book to feel more comfortable speaking in front of people. Chances are, you will give many oral presentations throughout your life, even as an adult! Businesspeople, scientists, politicians, reporters on television, teachers, and more all use oral presentations to explain ideas to other people.

The world's longest speech by one person was **77 hours** long.

Up to **75 percent** of people are afraid of giving oral presentations.

Visit the library to learn more about a subject.

To prepare for a presentation, you need to plan, **research**, write, and **rehearse**. Before you can begin these steps, you need to choose a **topic**. Sometimes you will be given a topic. Other times, you can choose your own. Anita's teacher asks his students to each do a presentation about being healthy. They can choose what particular topic they want to work on. As Anita takes a bite from a crisp apple, she knows her answer right away—teeth!

There are a lot of things to learn about health.

Try This

Choosing your own topic can be exciting! Start by listing six topics that interest you. They can be familiar topics or things that you want to learn more about. Next, take a close look at the topics you listed. Some might be just right for a short presentation. Others may be too broad. Narrow down any broad topics by focusing on a specific part.

FOR EXAMPLE:
Too broad: Basketball players
More specific: Michael Jordan

Too broad: Swimming
More specific: The four common swimming strokes

History of Oral Presentations

100 BC Famous speakers like Cicero give oral presentations as part of ancient Roman government meetings.

95 AD Roman speaker Quintilian writes a series of textbooks on being a convincing presenter.

1775 Strong oral presenters convince the American colonies to fight for independence from Britain. Patrick Henry gives his famous "Give Me Liberty or Give Me Death!" speech.

1825 John Quincy Adams, who had been a college teacher on oral presentation, becomes the sixth U.S. president.

1863 Abraham Lincoln gives the Gettysburg Address, which begins with "Fourscore and seven years ago . . . "

1870s Susan B. Anthony goes on speaking tours across the United States to support women's right to vote.

1987 Computer company Microsoft releases PowerPoint, a program used to help speakers while giving oral presentations.

2018 Politician Nancy Pelosi's 8-hour talk sets the record for the longest speech given during a U.S. government meeting in more than 100 years.

Mapping Oral Presentations

Qunu, South Africa, 2013 - A funeral is held for former South African president Nelson Mandela. Mandela gave many historic speeches and oral presentations on equality and the struggle against racism around the world.

Rome, Italy, 500 AD - The Roman Forum becomes an important place for public events, including oral presentations.

2 Chapter Two

Planning Your Presentation

Once you know your topic, begin planning your presentation. The word PLAN can help you remember four things to think about when planning a presentation.

Purpose: Why are you presenting this topic? Some presentations give information, such as Anita's presentation on healthy teeth. Other presentations can be persuasive, such as trying to convince people to recycle.

Length: How long is your presentation supposed to be? Anita knows hers should be three to four minutes long. She will need to choose the most important parts of her topic. If you have a longer presentation, you can add more details.

Audience: Who will be listening to your presentation? What do they already know about the topic? Which details should be included to help them understand your presentation?

P urpose
L ength
A udience
N otes and Visual Aids

Anita's friend Zack is presenting in his class about the animals that live in each layer of the rain forest. Because the class already studied rain forest layers, he can focus on the animals without spending much time explaining the layers. What if his class had not studied rain forest layers yet? Then he would need to include some information about the layers so his classmates could understand where the animals live.

Notes and Visual Aids: What items are you allowed to use in your presentation? You will probably be able to use notes, but check to make sure. Also, find out if you can use **visual aids** such as pictures, maps, or posters. Anita's teacher asked his students to use some technology, such as slide shows and videos.

Your audience will probably be made up of your classmates and teachers.

Try This

There are many types of visual aids. You want to choose visual aids that help the audience understand your topic. On a separate piece of paper, match each purpose listed on the left with the visual aid on the right. Turn this page upside down to compare your answers to ours.

TOPIC: Australia

Purpose:

1. Learn where Australian cities are located
2. See what money is used in Australia
3. Learn how Australians throw boomerangs
4. See the pouches of Australian animals

Visual Aid:

A. Pass around Australian coins

B. Show photos of kangaroos and koalas

C. Display on map

D. Play a video

Answers: 1. C 2. A 3. D 4. B

3 Chapter Three

Research and Write

For any presentation, you want your information to be correct. To do this, you should research your topic. This is a good idea even if you already know a lot about your topic. Websites, books, and experts on your topic can be good sources of information. Librarians are research specialists, so your school and public library are great places to go if you need help. When Anita looks for information, her dad helps her do some research online. They also visit the library.

Once you have enough information, it is time to write a draft. Organize your presentation into three parts: **introduction**, **body**, and **conclusion**. The introduction, or beginning, introduces your topic. Use an interesting fact or a joke in your introduction to grab the audience's attention. The body, or middle, contains information about your topic. Keep the length of your presentation in mind when adding details. The longer your presentation, the more facts you will need. Anita has to limit how many facts she includes because her presentation must be short. The conclusion, or ending, summarizes your presentation. It will help the audience remember the presentation's main points.

When your draft is finished, you don't want to read it word for word. If you read directly from your paper, it is hard to speak loudly and make eye contact with the audience. Instead, you should make notes. For her notes, Anita writes key words and phrases on note cards. She can look down at the note cards to help her remember what to say. Then, she can look up and speak to the audience.

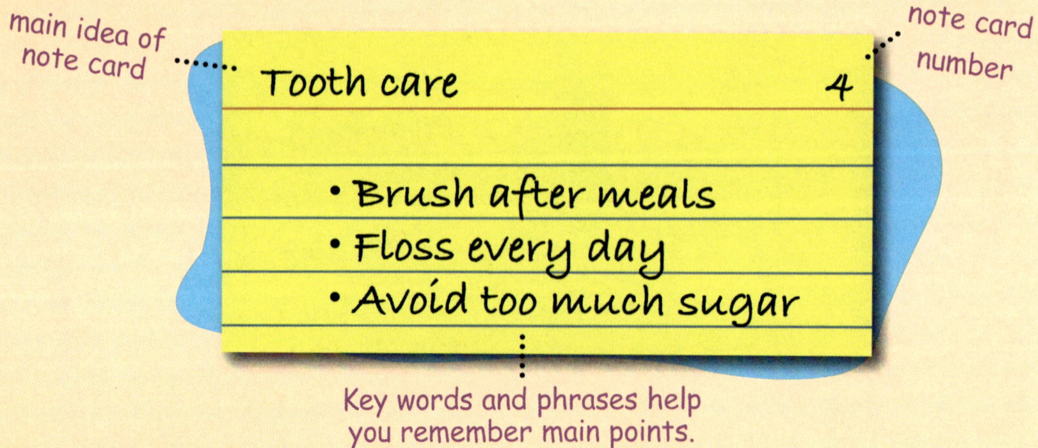

Try This

Read the following information about German shepherds. On a note card, write down several key words or phrases about what makes them good pets. Turn the page upside down to compare your notes to ours.

German shepherds make excellent pets. They are great watchdogs, since they are naturally protective of their families. These dogs get along well with children. German shepherds are also very easy to train.

4 Chapter Four

Practice Makes Perfect

Before you take the stage, it is a good idea to rehearse, or practice. Give your presentation in front of a mirror. You can also record it on video and watch it. Time yourself to see if your presentation is too long or too short. Practice these skills that good speakers use:

- Speak in a loud, clear voice so that the audience can hear you.
- Look up from your note cards and make eye contact with the audience.
- Use expression and **gestures**. If you seem bored with your topic, the audience will feel the same way.

Many people say "um" and "you know" when they speak. People use these **fillers** when they are trying to think of the right words to use. However, these phrases can be distracting to the audience. The more you practice your presentation, the less you will need to stop and think.

Anita practices several times by herself first. Then she rehearses her presentation in front of her family and friends. She asks them to time her. When she finishes, she asks them for suggestions to improve her presentation.

Try This

Ask someone to videotape you giving a presentation or telling a story. When you have finished, watch the video. Copy the chart below on a separate piece of paper. Use this to help you reflect on your performance.

In my presentation, I...	Not at all	Some	A lot
Spoke loudly and clearly			
Made eye contact			
Used fillers ("um", "you know")			
Spoke with expression			
Used gestures			

Discuss your answers with the person who took the video. How would he or she rate your performance? Which skills did you do well? Which ones need improvement?

5 Chapter Five

Presentation Time!

The day of the presentation is here. Anita knows it is normal to be nervous before presenting to a group. Even adults feel this way! She has confidence in herself. She worked hard at researching her topic, writing her notes, and rehearsing her presentation. Now it is time to enjoy her moment in the spotlight!

When you present, take time to prepare. Check that you have everything you need. Have your note cards in order and your visual aids ready. Take a few deep breaths. Breathing in and out slowly will relax your nerves and help you speak in a calm, clear voice.

When someone is done presenting, be sure to give them a round of applause.

During your presentation, be confident. Keep in mind the tips you practiced: speak clearly, make eye contact with the audience, and use expression and gestures. Many people rush through their presentations. Be sure to take your time so that the audience can understand your words and visual aids. Remember, you have worked hard to prepare for this. Go up there and have fun!

When you finish presenting, ask the audience if they have any questions. If you don't know the answer to a question, be honest and say that you don't know. You may be an expert on your topic, but you're not expected to know everything. Thank the audience for listening and enjoy the applause!

Martin Luther King Jr. gave his "I Have a Dream" speech in front of **250,000 people**.

The longest speech given by a team of people went on for **126 hours and 28 minutes**.

Try This

With the help of an adult, search online for videos of famous speeches. Martin Luther King Jr.'s "I Have a Dream" speech and President John F. Kennedy's "We Choose to Go to the Moon" speech are examples of powerful oral presentations. Which skills from this book do the speakers use in their speeches?

Martin Luther King Jr.'s speeches helped change history.

Quiz

1
What are some types of people who use oral presentations?

2
What do you need to do to prepare for a presentation?

3
Which U.S. president was also a college teacher on oral presentation?

4
How can you keep from seeming bored with your topic while giving a presentation?

5
How long was Nancy Pelosi's 2018 speech?

6
What does the word PLAN stand for?

7
What are the three parts of a presentation?

8
What are some examples of visual aids?

9
How many people did Martin Luther King Jr. give his "I Have a Dream" speech in front of?

10
What should you do when you finish presenting?

Answers: 1. Businesspeople, scientists, politicians, reporters on television, and teachers **2.** Plan, research, write, and rehearse **3.** John Quincy Adams **4.** Use expressions and gestures **5.** 8 hours **6.** Purpose, Length, Audience, and Notes and Visual Aids **7.** Introduction, body, and conclusion **8.** Pictures, maps, posters, a slideshow, and videos **9.** 250,000 **10.** Ask the audience if they have any questions.

Key Words

body: the middle of a presentation that includes details about the topic

conclusion: the ending of a presentation that summarizes the main points

fillers: words or phrases people say when they pause to think during a presentation

gestures: hand or body movements that help express an idea

introduction: the beginning of a presentation that contains the main idea and grabs the audience's attention

oral presentation: a short talk a person gives to a group about a certain topic

rehearse: to practice before presenting to an audience

research: to collect information about a topic

topic: the subject of a discussion, study, lesson, speech, or piece of writing

visual aids: objects the audience can see that help them understand a presentation

Index

audiences 5, 10, 11, 12, 14, 16, 19, 21

body 14, 21
breathing 18

conclusions 14, 21
confidence 18, 19

drafts 14

expressions 16, 17, 19, 21
eye contact 14, 16, 17, 19

facts 14
fillers 16, 17

gestures 16, 17, 19, 21

introduction 14

jokes 14

Kennedy, President John F. 20
key words 14, 15
King, Martin Luther, Jr. 19, 20, 21

length 10, 14, 21
librarians 13

nervousness 5, 18
notes 11, 14, 15, 16, 18, 21

planning 6, 10, 21
practice 16, 19
purpose 10, 12, 21

questions 19, 21

research 6, 13, 18, 21

topics 6, 7, 10, 12, 13, 14, 16, 18, 19, 21

videos 11, 12, 16, 17, 20, 21
visual aids 10, 11, 12, 18, 19, 21

writing 6, 8, 13, 14, 15, 18, 21

LIGHTBOX

SUPPLEMENTARY RESOURCES

Click on the plus icon found in the bottom left corner of each spread to open additional teacher resources.

- Download and print the book's quizzes and activities
- Access curriculum correlations
- Explore additional web applications that enhance the Lightbox experience

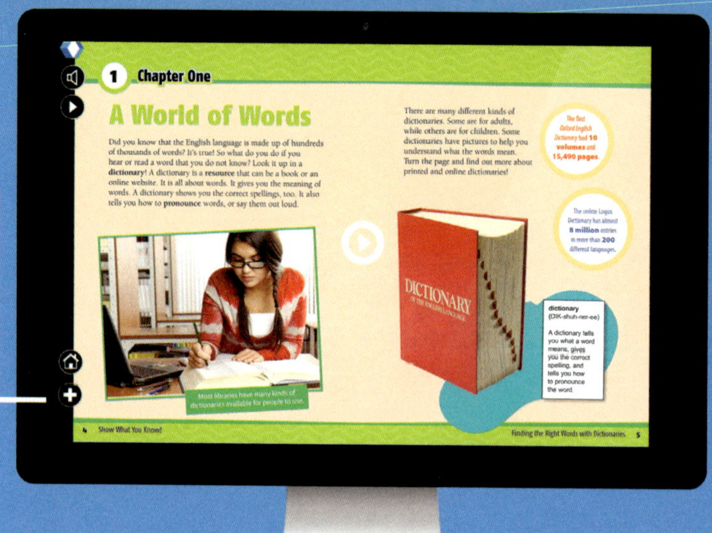

LIGHTBOX DIGITAL TITLES
Packed full of integrated media

VIDEOS

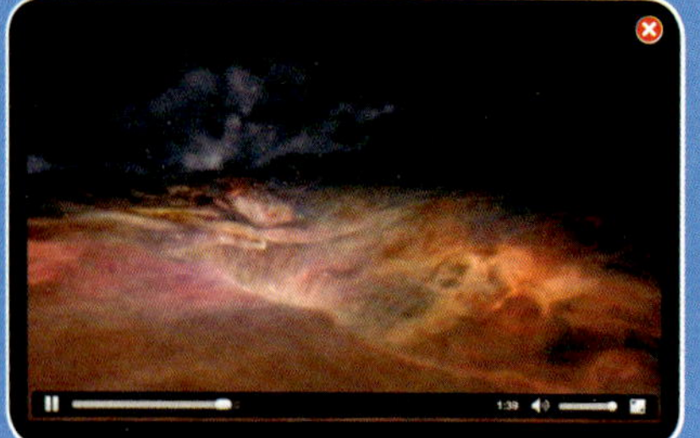

INTERACTIVE MAPS

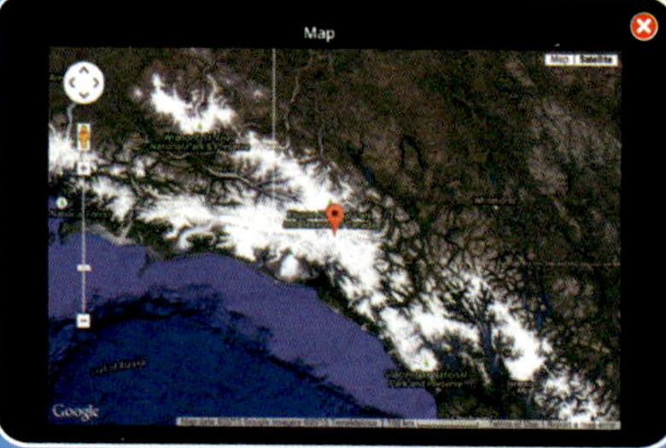

WEBLINKS

SLIDESHOWS

QUIZZES

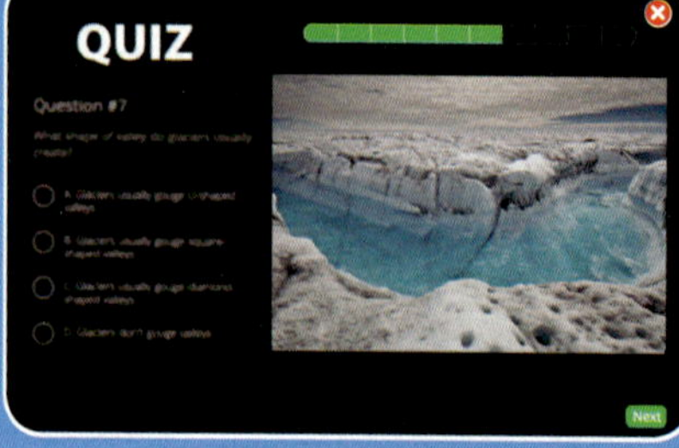

OPTIMIZED FOR

- ✓ TABLETS
- ✓ WHITEBOARDS
- ✓ COMPUTERS
- ✓ AND MUCH MORE!

Published by Smartbook Media Inc. 350 5th Avenue, 59th Floor New York, NY 10118
Website: www.openlightbox.com

First published by Cherry Lake Publishing in 2013

Library of Congress Control Number: 2018941477

ISBN 978-1-5105-3977-8 (hardcover)
ISBN 978-1-5105-3978-5 (multi-user eBook)

Printed in Brainerd, Minnesota, United States
1 2 3 4 5 6 7 8 9 0 22 21 20 19 18

062018
120517

Project Coordinator Heather Kissock
Designer Nick Newton

Photo Credits
Every reasonable effort has been made to trace ownership and to obtain permission to reprint copyright material. The publisher would be pleased to have any errors or omissions brought to its attention so that they may be corrected in subsequent printings.

The publisher acknowledges Getty Images, Shutterstock, Alamy, and iStock as its primary image suppliers for this title.